Cla

THE PREHISTORIC WORLD OF THE DINOSAURS
TYRANNOSAURUS REX

First published in Great Britain in 1993 by
Boxtree Limited, Broadwall House, 21 Broadwall,
London SE1 9PL

Text copyright © 1993 David Taylor
Illustrations copyright © 1993 Boxtree Limited
All rights reserved

1 3 5 7 9 10 8 6 4 2

Illustrator: Wayne Ford
Editor: Miranda Smith
Designer: Anita Ruddell

1 85283 039 5

Typeset by Intype, London
Printed and bound in Belgium by Proost

Except in the United States of America, this book
is sold subject to the condition that it shall not by way
of trade or otherwise, be lent, resold, hired out or
otherwise circulated without the publisher's prior
consent in any form of binding or cover other than that
in which it is published and without a similar condition
including this condition being imposed on a subsequent
purchaser

A CIP catalogue record for this book is available from
the British Library

THE PREHISTORIC WORLD OF THE DINOSAURS
TYRANNOSAURUS REX

DAVID TAYLOR

BOXTREE

INTRODUCTION

The Earth is some 4,000 million years old and the first living things, bacteria, made their appearance in the ancient seas 3,000 million years ago. From then right up to the present day, a succession of animal types, each type more complex and advanced than that preceding it, have been, for a time, the masters of the planet and lords of a particular age in the history of evolution.

During the Age of Reptiles, a unique and fascinating kind of reptile arose. They were characterised by a special limb anatomy that enabled them to walk and

run more efficiently than other reptiles. These were the dinosaurs. They appeared about 225 million years ago, and vanished rather suddenly and mysteriously 180 million years later.

While the dinosaurs lived, they were worthy rulers of Earth. Some were peaceable plant-eaters, grazers on grass and browsers in trees. Others were the fiercest, most bloodthirsty creatures ever seen on Earth. The most fearsome of these "terrible lizards" was Tyrannosaurus rex.

THE TYRANT LIZARD

Tyrannosaurus rex is probably the most well-known of the dinosaurs. Its name means "tyrant lizard", and it was the king of its species.

Tyrannosaurus rex was the largest member of a fierce family group known as the tyrannosaurids, a group that included Albertosaurus and Daspletosaurus. However, Tyrannosaurus rex was the most

ferocious, not only of the tyrannosaurids, but of all the meat-eating dinosaurs. A fully-grown male was about 14 metres in length and weighed an incredible 7 tonnes. Its teeth were like long, sharp, hunting knives. Even the Deinosuchus, a giant early crocodile, would have slipped quickly into the waters of its marshy home if it saw a Tyrannosaurus rex coming its way!

Tyrannosaurus rex's massive head was supported by a powerful neck

Head in the clouds
A fully-grown Tyrannosaurus rex standing on its hind legs was an awesome sight. It towered to a height of around 5.5 metres, 1.2 metres higher than a double-decker bus!

Bipeds
Tyrannosaurus rex walked and even ran on its two hind legs, which were thick and pillar-like. Dinosaurs, unlike any other kind of reptile, had legs set under their bodies. This allowed them to run fast.

The dinosaur's back legs each had three forward-pointing toes and one backward-pointing "spur"

Deinosuchus

This ancient crocodile was 12-13 metres long and probably preyed on dinosaurs. Its name means "terrible crocodile". The 25 species of modern crocodilians are the closest living relatives of the dinosaurs.

A strong framework

Fossils of Tyrannosaurus rex's skull, jaws, backbone, shoulders and limbs have been found. A fully grown male would have been 14 metres long and weighed 7 tonnes. A long tail would have been necessary to act as a counterweight to balance the heavy front of the body when the creature was moving.

No fossil tailbones have been found

Life on land

Over 300 million years ago, the first newt-like creatures left the sea to feed on the worms and insects they found there. But early amphibians like the Ichthyostega had to return to the water to lay their eggs. From these early amphibians evolved the reptiles.

Ichthyostega

A WARM AND SUNNY LAND

100 million years ago, when Tyrannosaurus lived on the Earth, everywhere was warm and sunny, and the sea was like a warm bath. Volcanoes rumbled and there was the whiff of sulphur on the breeze. There were forests, woods, marshes and lakes. Among the ferns in the shady places and across the grassy water-meadows, all kinds of flowers bloomed. Bees and butterflies, pterosaurs and birds flew in the air; fish and turtles, crocodiles and plesiosaurs swam in the water; and an amazing variety of animals ranging from tiny mammals to enormous dinosaurs roamed the land.

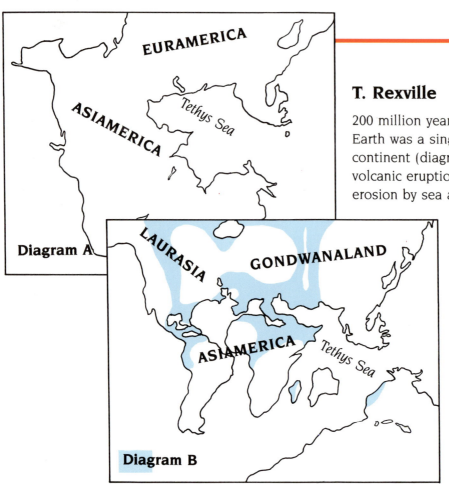

Diagram A

Diagram B

T. Rexville

200 million years ago, all land on the Earth was a single enormous super-continent (diagram A). As time passed, volcanic eruptions, earthquakes and erosion by sea and storms caused the super-continent to break up. By the Age of the Dinosaurs, there were two new continents, Asiamerica and Euramerica (diagram B).

Thecodonts

Thecodonts appeared 220 million years ago. At first, they were crocodile-like animals, such as Erythrosuchus, that walked on four legs. Later animals walked on two legs. From the thecodonts, four main groups of creatures evolved: the crocodiles; the "reptile-hipped" dinosaurs like Tyrannosaurus rex and all other carnivorous dinosaurs; the "bird-hipped" dinosaurs who were herbivorous; and the flying reptiles.

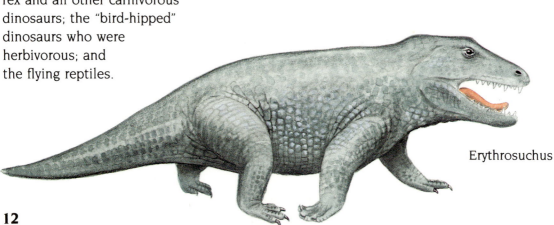

Megozostrodon

Erythrosuchus

Dinosaur hips

Dinosaur hips were of two different shapes. "Reptile-hipped" dinosaurs included large plant-eaters such as Diplodocus and meat-eaters such as Tyrannosaurus rex.

"Bird-hipped" dinosaurs were plant-eaters such as Triceratops and the ankylosaurids.

Reptile-hipped dinosaur

Bird-hipped dinosaur

Mammals

The first mammal-like reptiles evolved about 290 million years ago. True mammals, like Megazostrodon, probably came on the scene just after the first dinosaurs. They were small, insect-eating creatures very similar to today's shrews. Mammals are warm-blooded, have hair and give birth to live young which they suckle on milk.

A warm climate

When the first dinosaurs appeared, ferns, horsetails, coniferous trees, cycads and maidenhair trees grew on the land, but no grass or flowering plants. By the time of Tyrannosaurus rex this had changed and there were species which looked like today's cinnamon, eucalyptus, oak, walnut, poplar, holly and pistachio nut trees. There were also figs, willows, magnolias and ivy.

Gingko

Horsetails

Tree fern

Magnolia

Cycad

AT THE WATER'S EDGE

Tyrannosaurus rex's dramatic snarls would have bared incredible teeth to the world. The mere sight of this dinosaur bursting out of the horsetails would have been enough to scare away the many creatures that lived on the edge of the warm seas. There, flocks of the pelican-like waterbirds, Hesperornis, hunted for bony fish with their long, sharp-toothed beaks, and the giant turtle, Archelon, rooted for clams and snails in the sand.

Tyrannosaurus rex would have been annoyed by the teasing of the gaggles of pterosaurs that swooped down from the cliff edges to spear fish, but could have done little to stop them. And although Tyrannosaurus was able to move fast, it would still not have been quick enough to catch the tiny hairy mammals that scuttled in the undergrowth beneath its feet. This enormous and fierce predator had its sights fixed on larger prey.

Flying reptiles

The flying pterosaurs were reptiles, not birds. The largest, Quetzalcoatlus, had a wingspan of 15 metres, as broad as many jet fighter planes. Pterosaurs did not have feathers, but were probably hairy, their coats insulating them against the cold. Some pterosaurs had bony crests on top of their heads which may have served as counterweights when their beaks were tilted down to take food on the wing.

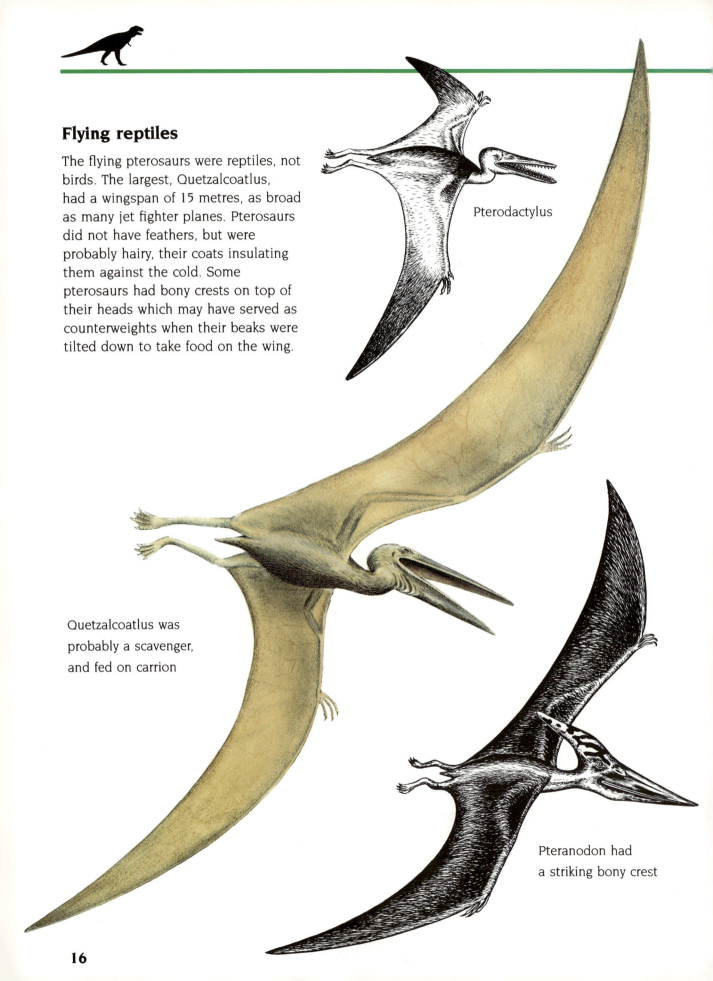

Pterodactylus

Quetzalcoatlus was probably a scavenger, and fed on carrion

Pteranodon had a striking bony crest

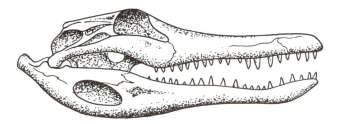

Crocodile skull

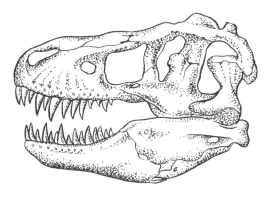

Tyrannosaurus rex skull

All teeth

Crocodiles are tight-lipped with the thin skin of their faces fixed firmly to the bone beneath. They cannot snarl or bare their teeth. Lizards, however, can. Their skulls are provided with lines of holes beneath the lips through which pass the blood vessels and nerves that control the muscles for lip movement. Tyrannosaurus rex probably could snarl as it had identical lip holes.

Giant turtles

Archelon was a gigantic animal, growing to almost 4 metres in length. Its thick, hard shell protected it from predators. Archelon had a horny beak and weak jaws, and may have preferred a diet of jellyfish when available.

A FIERCE PREDATOR

The favourite hunting-grounds of Tyrannosaurus rex were the open grazing areas of low ferns where it could catch ornithomimosaurs (ostrich dinosaurs) and dromaeosaurids (running reptile dinosaurs). However, its favourite food was an easy prey, the hadrosaurs. These duck-billed dinosaurs were plant-eaters, cropping ferns and ginkgo trees by the water's edge. It is probable that they could be heard whistling and hooting as they browsed. Tyrannosaurus rex would have had to ambush or charge them, because if they had had time to reach the water they would have escaped. Unlike Tyrannosaurus, which was only capable of wading, the hadrosaurs were designed to swim quite well, with their deep tails and paddle-like forepaws.

Ornithomimosaurs

These creatures did look rather like ostriches. They were up to 4 metres long, and usually stood and ran upright. They had long necks and small heads with toothless, horny beaks. Ornithomimosaurs such as Gallimimus could probably run fast to catch prey or escape predators – perhaps, like the ostrich, reaching 48 kph or more.

Gallimimus

Dromaeosaurids

Running reptile dinosaurs only measured up to 3.5 metres long and 2 metres tall. But they were fierce meat-eaters. They probably hunted in packs. Deinonychus ("terrible claw"), was a swift dromaeosaurid with over 70 sharp teeth and a long stabbing claw on each foot.

Deinonychus

Duck-billed dinosaurs

Hadrosaurs were 4–13 metres long with powerfully-arched backs, heavy hind legs and much smaller front legs. They all had duck-like beaks, but their heads were all kinds of shapes. Hadrosaurs were plant-eaters that often stood more or less upright on their hind legs to reach the leaves of trees like conifers. They had rows of hundreds of grinding teeth with which they chewed the tough plant fibre.

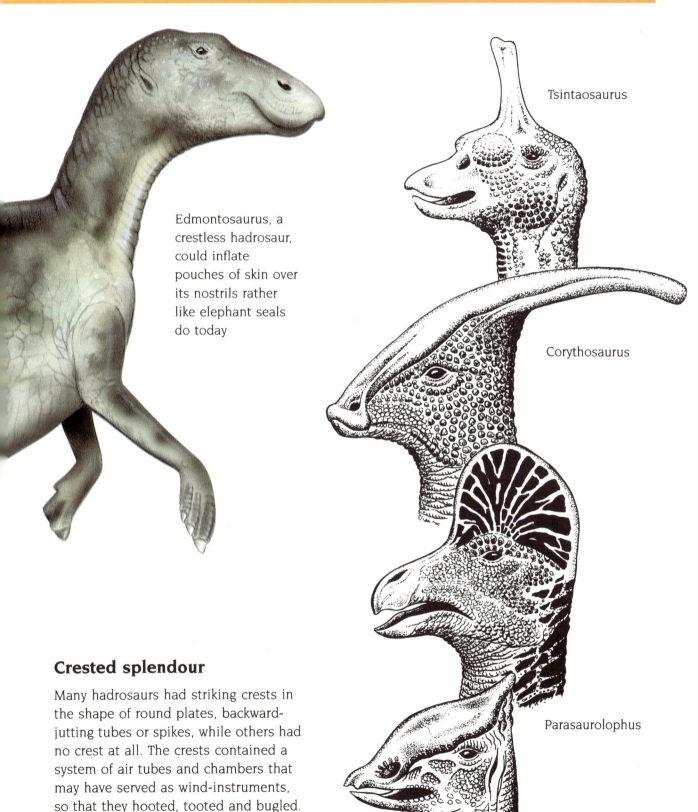

Edmontosaurus, a crestless hadrosaur, could inflate pouches of skin over its nostrils rather like elephant seals do today

Tsintaosaurus

Corythosaurus

Parasaurolophus

Saurolophus

Crested splendour

Many hadrosaurs had striking crests in the shape of round plates, backward-jutting tubes or spikes, while others had no crest at all. The crests contained a system of air tubes and chambers that may have served as wind-instruments, so that they hooted, tooted and bugled. The crests were probably brightly coloured so the animals could recognize others of the same species.

ARMED COMBAT

Tyrannosaurus rex's body was built for combat. Its massive head, with a skull far heavier than those of other dinosaurs, could be used as a deadly battering ram and its 20 centimetre-long teeth would have ripped prey apart in minutes. There were very few creatures able to stand up to such a creature, but an Ankylosaur was able to fight back! Its armoured skin protected it from the bites of a foe and it could have whirled round and clouted attackers with the club on the end of its tail. By swinging its tail backwards and forwards in this way it could have easily beaten off predators like Tyrannosaurus rex.

The Triceratops were rhinoceros-like creatures who grazed in herds on the open plains. They were also capable of defending themselves, but being placid plant-eaters, they would normally have avoided Tyrannosaurus rex if they saw him coming. If trapped, they would form a circle with their horns jutting outwards, and those nearest to the attacker would lunge and charge, trying to impale it.

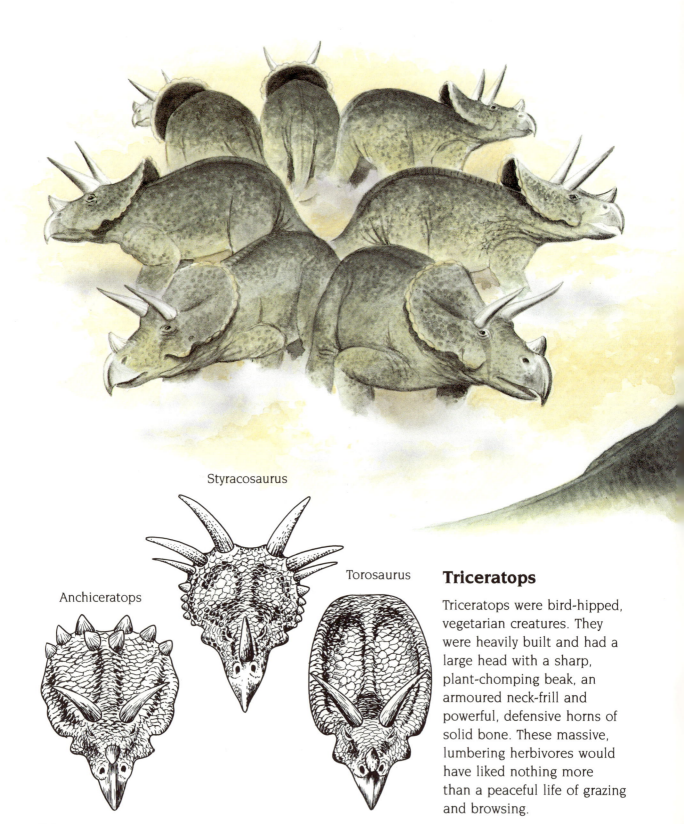

Styracosaurus

Anchiceratops

Torosaurus

Triceratops

Triceratops were bird-hipped, vegetarian creatures. They were heavily built and had a large head with a sharp, plant-chomping beak, an armoured neck-frill and powerful, defensive horns of solid bone. These massive, lumbering herbivores would have liked nothing more than a peaceful life of grazing and browsing.

Under threat

Triceratops lived in herds, and when threatened, behaved in the way a group of buffalo do today when confronted by a predator. They made a defensive circle, horned and frilled heads facing outwards in the direction of the threat. Such a wall of jutting, pronged heads would make a formidable barrier.

Tyrannosaurus rex had a short, thick neck

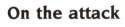

On the attack

The skull of Tyrannosaurus rex was solid and heavy, and its powerful spine was designed to cope with sudden intense pressure travelling down its length. These features indicate that the dinosaur had evolved as a sort of high-speed battering ram. It would charge at its prey at a speed of up to 32 kph and when the jaws slammed into the Triceratops or hadrosaur, Tyrannosaurus rex's skull was the first part of the body to take the shock.

Ankylosaurids

These dinosaurs were "bird-hipped" vegetarians that resembled medieval knights carrying spiked maces or iron balls. In the case of ankylosaurids, the weapons were one or more lumps of bone, rounded in shape, set at the extreme tip of their tails. They had heavy, bony body armour, walked on all fours and measured up to a massive 6 metres in length.

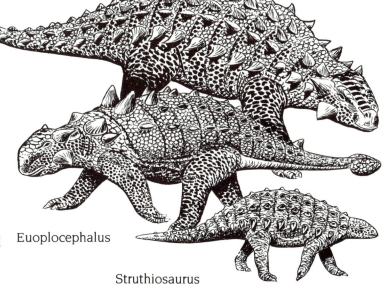

Ankylosaurus

Euoplocephalus

Struthiosaurus

THE END OF THE DINOSAURS?

At the end of the age of the dinosaurs, an asteroid streaked out of space and collided with the Earth. The Earth shuddered and great trees crashed to the ground. The sun danced in the sky and then suddenly was gone. The sky became black and there was the darkness of early night, but no moon or stars, just the glow of volcanoes. And there was a smell of hot dust and burning.

A great wall of sea water swept across the marsh and ferny land, leaving behind it the bodies of dead turtles, fish and sharks. Slowly the air grew colder and gradually those creatures still alive began to die. Only the little scuttling mammals, that had been hiding underground when disaster struck, emerged from their holes to root for food in the wasteland.

Impact!

Asteroids are lumps of rock in orbit round the Sun. There are literally millions of them, some no bigger than an apple, others 20 kms in diameter. Should the orbit of an asteroid cross that of the Earth as it, too, moves round the Sun, a collision is possible. Because these pieces of space junk travel at about 80,000 kph, the effect of the impact is devastating. An asteroid 100 metres in diameter would blast a crater 2 kms across and 100 metres deep – similar to the hole created by just such an event 40,000 years ago in Arizona, USA. Asteroids 1 km across hit the Earth on average every 100,000 years while giant ones, 20 kms across, hit every 10 to 100 million years or so.

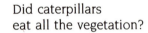

Did caterpillars eat all the vegetation?

The end of an era

There are many theories about why the dinosaurs died out. All the alternative theories have their weak points, and the arguments continue. Some of the theories are as follows:

1. The dinosaurs starved to death because moth and butterfly caterpillars ate most of the vegetation.
2. The mammals fed on dinosaur eggs.
3. The dinosaurs were poisoned by some of the new kinds of plants that evolved.
4. There was an epidemic.
5. The gradual warming of the Earth caused cataracts that affected the eyes of the dinosaurs and blinded them.
6. The dinosaurs died because of intense radiation coming from outer space.

Did mammals like Megazastrodon eat the dinosaurs' eggs?

The dark of night

There would have been an unimaginable explosion as the asteroid landed and was blown to smithereens. A pall of dust would have been cast up into the atmosphere that would have persisted for months. Darkness would have descended on the land and plant life, denied sunlight, would have died, followed shortly afterwards by the animals that fed on it and, in turn, by the predators that fed on them.

GLOSSARY

aquatic Living in the water.
amphibian A cold-blooded, smooth-skinned creature that begins life in water but can live on land.
ankylosaurids A group of plant-eating dinosaurs with a tough armoured skin.
archosaurs A major group of reptiles that included the dinosaurs, pterosaurs and thecodonts.
biped An animal with two feet.
carnivorous Meat-eating.
ceratopid A group of plant-eating dinosaurs with bony horns.
descendant An animal or plant descended from an earlier form in the same species.
dromaeosaurids A group of fast-running, meat-eating dinosaurs.
evolution A gradual process by which a plant or animal changes into a different form, usually more complex.
fossils The ancient remains of an animal or plant that have been found in the earth.
hadrosaurs A group of dinosaurs that had webbed feet and a ducklike bill.
herbivorous Plant-eating.
mammals Warm-blooded hairy animals which feed their young on milk.
migration A move from one place to another, in search of food or warmer conditions.
pedigree An animal's family tree.
plesiosaurs A group of large, long-necked reptiles that lived in the sea at the same time as the dinosaurs lived on Earth.
predator An animal that lives by hunting and eating other animals.
prey An animal that is hunted and eaten by other animals.
pterosaurs Flying reptiles that lived at the time of the dinosaurs.
reptile A cold-blooded scaly animal such as the snake, lizard or dinosaur whose young are hatched from eggs with shells.
species A group of animals or plants which have the same characteristics and can breed together.
thecodonts A group of meat-eating ancestors of the dinosaurs.
vertebrate A creature that has a backbone and a bony skeleton within its body.

Albertosaurus
(al-bert-oh-saw-rus)
Length: 9 m
Meat-eater

Ankylosaurus
(an-ky-low-saw-rus)
Length: 10 m
Plant-eater

Archelon
(ark-a-lon)
Length: 3.7 m
Jellyfish and shellfish-eater

Cynognathus
(syne-og-nay-thus)
Length: 1.8 m
Meat-eater

Daspletosaurus
(da-spleet-oh-saw-rus)
Length: 9 m
Meat-eater

Deinonychus
(die-no-nike-us)
Length: 3 m
Meat-eater

INDEX

Age of Dinosaurs 12
Age of Reptiles 4
Albertosaurus 6, 30
amphibians 9
Anchiceratops 24
ankylosaurids 13, 22, 25
Ankylosaurus 25, 30
Archelon 14, 17, 30
asteroid impact 28–29
bird-hipped dinosaurs 12, 13, 24
caterpillars 28
Corythosaurus 21
crocodiles 9, 12, 17
Cycognathus 30
Daspletosaurus 6, 30
Deinonychus 20, 30
Deinosuchus 7, 9, 31
dinosaurs 5, 29
   death of 28–29
   eggs 29
Edmontosaurus 20–21, 31
Euoplocephalus 25
Euramerica 12
flying reptiles 12, 16,
fossils 17
hadrosaurs 18, 20–21
   crests 21
Ichthyostega 9, 31
lizards 17
mammal-like reptiles 13
mammals 13, 15, 29
meat-eaters 7
Megazastrodon 12, 13, 29, 31
ostrich dinosaurs 19, 20
Parasaurolophus 21
plant-eaters 5, 7, 12, 22
plesiosaurs 10, 19
Pteranodon 16
Pterodactylus 16
Quetzalcoatlus 16
reptile-hipped dinosaurs 12, 13
reptiles 4, 8, 9
running-reptile dinosaurs 19, 20
Saurolophus 18, 21, 31
snakes 9
sharks 27
Struthiosaurus 25
Styracosaurus 24
thecondonts 12
Torosaurus 24
Triceratops 13, 23, 24–25, 31
Tsintaosaurus 21
tyrannosaurus 5, 10
   toes 8
   neck 8, 25
skull 25
spur 8
tail 9
teeth 7

Tyrannosaurus rex
(tie-ran-oh-saw-rus rex)
Length: 15 m
Meat-eater

Deinosuchus
(die-no-soo-kus)
Length: 15 m
Meat-eater

Edmontosaurus
(ed-mont-oh-saw-rus)
Length: 13 m
Plant-eater

Ichthyostega
(ik-the-oh-stay-ga)
Length: 1 m
Fish and meat-eater

Megazostrodon
(meg-a-zoss-troh-don)
Length: 12 cm
Insect-eater

Saurolophus
(sawr-oh-loaf-us)
Length: 9 m
Plant-eater

Triceratops
(try-ser-a-tops)
Length: 9 m
Plant-eater

THE AUTHOR

David Taylor is a well-known veterinary surgeon who works internationally on wild and often rare animals such as giant pandas, komodo dragons, gorillas and dolphins. During the course of his work he has been bitten by a monkey, clawed by a leopard, squashed by an elephant, kicked by camels and almost drowned by a killer whale. He has travelled the world, working in a total of 32 countries, treating everything from elephants with toothache to tigers with food-poisoning. David appears regularly on television and radio, and amazingly has found time to write over 30 books including eight volumes of autobiography.